SMART BRAIN RIGHT BRAIN

The Art of Mixing Colours

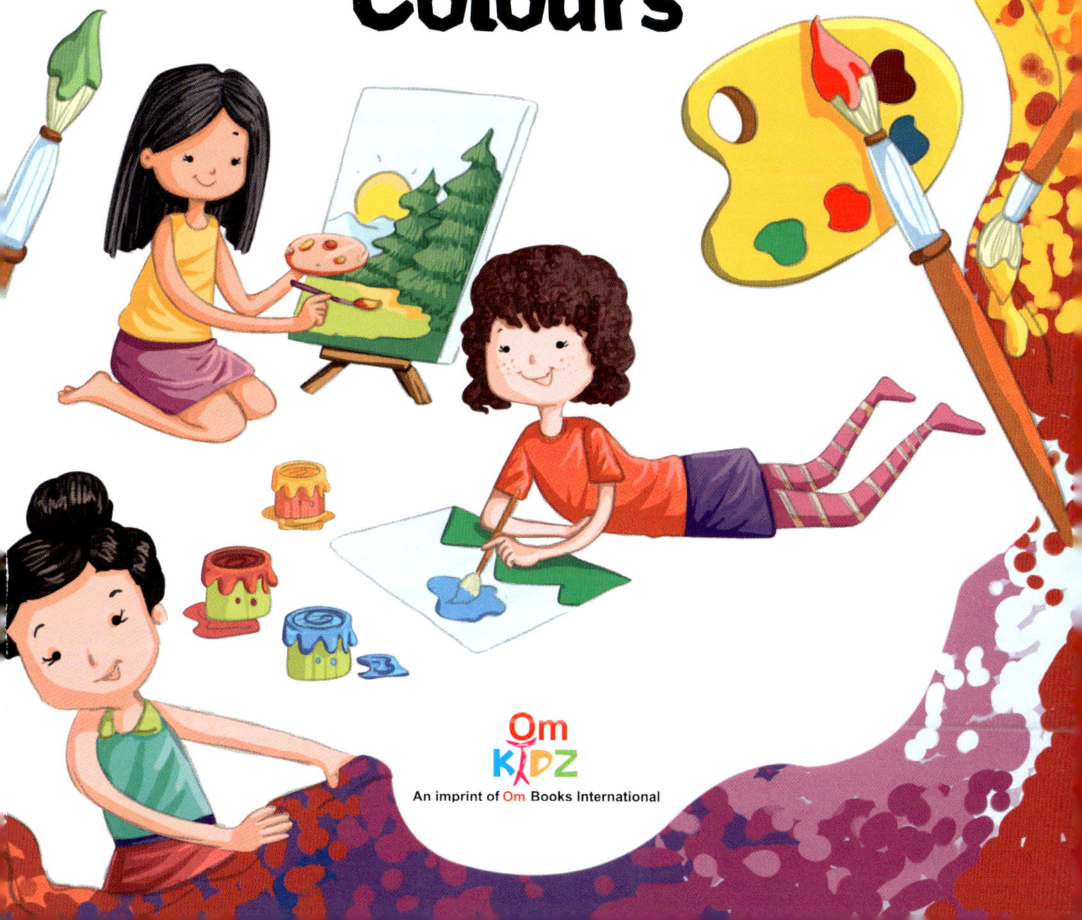

Om KIDZ
An imprint of Om Books International

Om Books International

Reprinted in 2023

Corporate & Editorial Office
A-12, Sector 64, Noida 201 301
Uttar Pradesh, India
Phone: +91 120 477 4100
Email: editorial@ombooks.com
Website: www.ombooksinternational.com

Sales Office
107, Ansari Road, Darya Ganj
New Delhi 110 002, India
Phone: +91 11 4000 9000
Email: sales@ombooks.com

Author: Swayam Ganguly
Editor: Nandita Bhardwaj
Art & Design: Anshuman Pandey, Gaurav Bhandari, Harish Arya

ISBN: 978-93-52768-48-6

Printed in India

10 9 8 7 6 5 4 3 2

CONTENTS

1. An Introduction to Colours

Our world is beautiful, energetic and extremely colourful. But imagine a world without any colours. Black trees instead of green, white rivers instead of blue, and colourless flowers! Wouldn't that be so dull and boring? Why, there would be no rainbow too! As colours are so important in our lives, don't you think it is important for us to know more about colours?

POCKET FACT

The word 'colours' was taken from the Latin word 'colos', which means 'a cover'.

Why are colours important?

Colours affect us in many ways, both mentally and physically. Some colours make you happy while others make you sad. A strong red colour may result in making you angry, while a blue colour can calm down an angry person.

DID YOU KNOW?

Many ancient cultures like the Egyptians and Chinese, practised chromotherapy, which means using colours to heal sick people.

How do colours help astronomers?

Astronomy is the study of the stars in the sky and the people who study them are called astronomers. Colours help astronomers identify the stars. The bluer a star, the bigger it is. The less blue and more yellowish a star is, the smaller it is. So, the next time you find yourself in front of a telescope, see which ones are the big stars, and which are the smaller stars. Remember, you have two colours to guide you – blue and yellow.

POCKET FACT

Just like maths and science, there are subjects that teach colours too. These studies are called chromatics, colorimetry, and chromatography.

2. Know Your Colours Better

Now, before you start mixing colours to create that wonderful drawing or painting that will impress everybody, you need to understand the qualities of the different colours that you will paint with and how they mix with one another. There are three types of colours – Primary, Secondary and Tertiary.

Primary Colours

Red, blue and yellow are the **Primary Colours** from which we get all the other colours. When we mix these three colours with one another in different proportions we get the other colours in the spectrum.

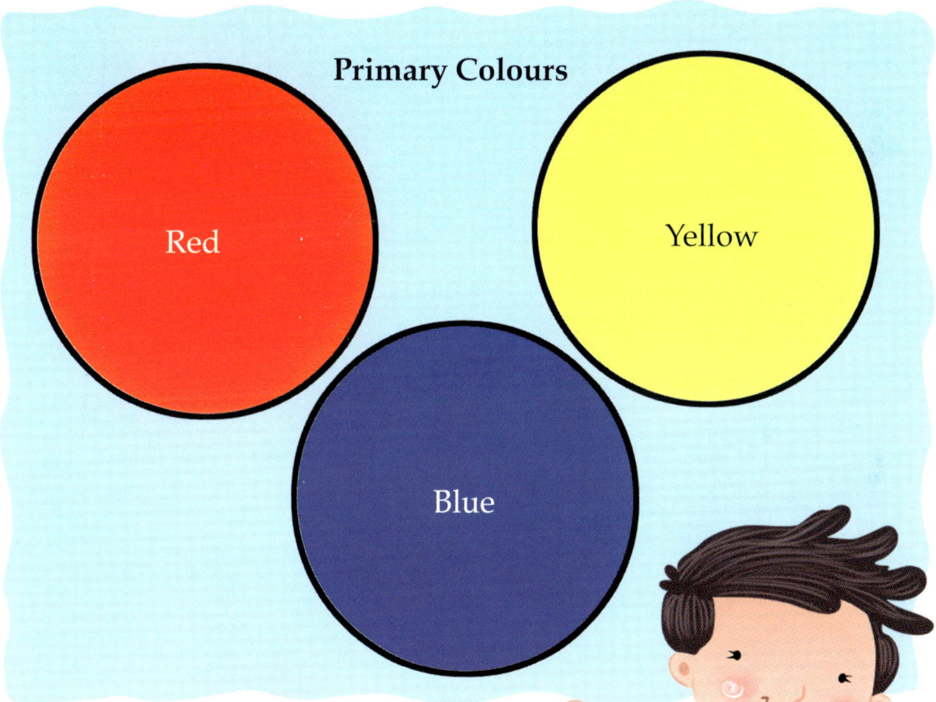

POCKET FACT

The three basic colours - red, blue, yellow - are the only colours that cannot be made by mixing other colours.

Secondary Colours

When we mix two primary colours, we get secondary colours. For example, when we mix red and blue, we get violet, and if we mix blue and yellow, green is produced. We get orange when red and yellow are mixed together.

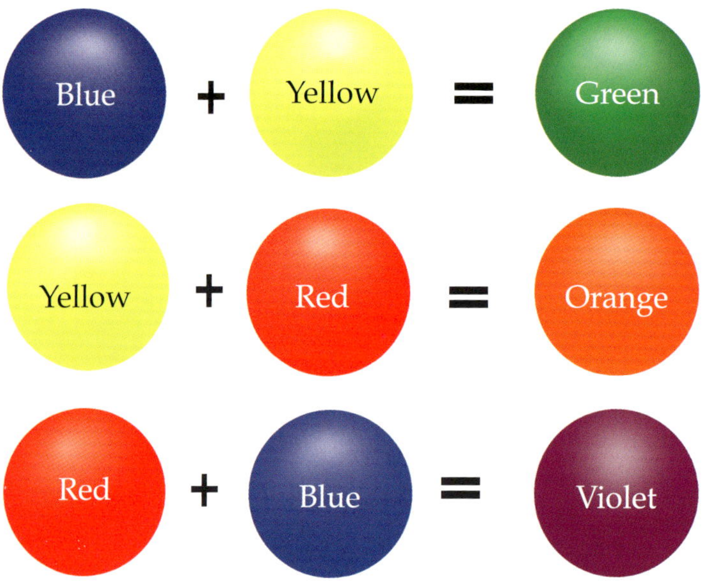

Red, blue, and yellow,
Three Primary Colours standing in a row.

Tertiary Colours

When we mix primary and secondary colours in equal parts or two secondary colours, we get **Tertiary Colours**. There are six tertiary colours: red-orange, yellow-orange, yellow-green, blue-green, blue-violet, and red-violet.

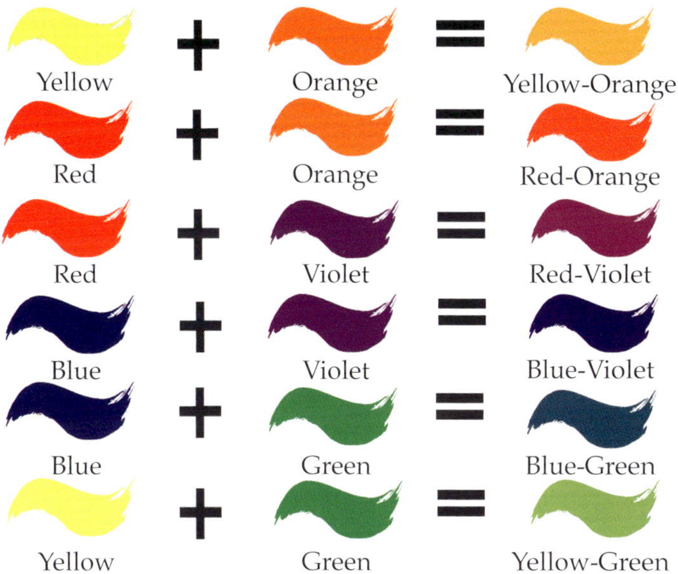

The tertiary colours have a lot of variety, and you can use them to suit your artwork or painting in different ways. For example, you could make a yellow-orange more yellow and less orange or a blue-green greener and less blue. Isn't that wonderful?

POCKET FACT

All tertiary colours are created by mixing a primary colour with a secondary colour. But when we mix two secondary colours together, we get colours like greys, browns and blacks.

3. Choosing the Right Colours

Choosing the right colours and mixing them correctly is what makes a good painter, as well as a great painting. For example, if Pablo Picasso hadn't chosen the right colours and used the right tones in his paintings, they wouldn't have been so famous. So, choose wisely!

Five lovely colours to create a scene,

Red, blue, yellow, orange and green.

DID YOU KNOW?

Some birds and animals recognise colour. Monkeys, many species of birds, fish and squirrels can distinguish one colour from another.

When you choose colours for mixing, begin with a few colours instead of too many. Slowly, increase the number of colours as you become better.

Colour, colour! Which colour should I choose?

Oh dear, I'm so confused! What should I use?

Oops! I made a mess mixing the reds with the blues,

Wish I knew the don'ts and the dos.

POCKET FACT

Colour is a property of light as seen by us.

4. Mixing Colours the Right Way

Your style, talent or technique is as important as your knowledge of mixing colours. Many of us use colours without thinking. As a result, our paintings become flat. The best idea is to begin with a few colours instead of mixing many. Stick with red, yellow, blue and white for a few weeks. As you learn the art of mixing and get better, you can increase the number of colours. Don't be afraid to make mistakes. Just have fun.

POCKET FACT

Just like you are afraid of the dark, some people are afraid of colours. This disease is called Chromatophobia.

Always add dark to light

When you are mixing colours, you only need a small amount of a dark colour to change a light colour. But you need a lot more of a light colour to change a dark one.

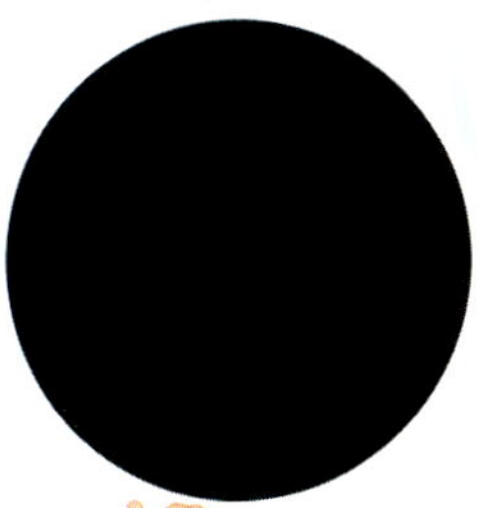

DID YOU KNOW?

There is a colour that we cannot see. The newly invented colour called 'Vantablack' is so dark that it looks as if it is a black hole!

POCKET FACT

If you want a darker shade, you can always add black to that colour. You can just add white to lighten a colour. But remember to use small amounts of black or white colour that you are using so that you get the right shade that you are looking for.

Black and white colour play

Some people think that white and black should come under primary colours and some others think that they should not. But what is important is that many black shades can be created by mixing other colours. However, no two colours can be mixed together to create white. But black and white do play an important role when you are mixing colours.

Hue, Value and Saturation

Any colour can be perceived in three dimensions- Hue, Value and Saturation.

Hue: Hue means the position of the colour on the colour wheel as well as its in-between colours. For example, as brown is a dark orange, orange is a hue of brown, and some of its intermediate colours are orange-red or orange-yellow. We combine colour pigments in order to get the required shades of a particular hue.

Value: The value of a colour shows how close it is to being either black or white. For example, yellow is a light colour and we can increase its lightness even more by adding white.

Saturation: The purity or intensity, or level of chroma of a colour is called saturation. Colours that have high saturation are the bright colours that you can see on a rainbow or a colour wheel. Colours that have less saturation are the dark colours or shades, muted colours or tones, and pale colours or tints.

The best way to learn more about mixing colours is to do it yourself and by keeping the above points in mind. So, go right ahead. Grab some colours and brushes and start mixing those colours. You can take the help of a colour wheel!

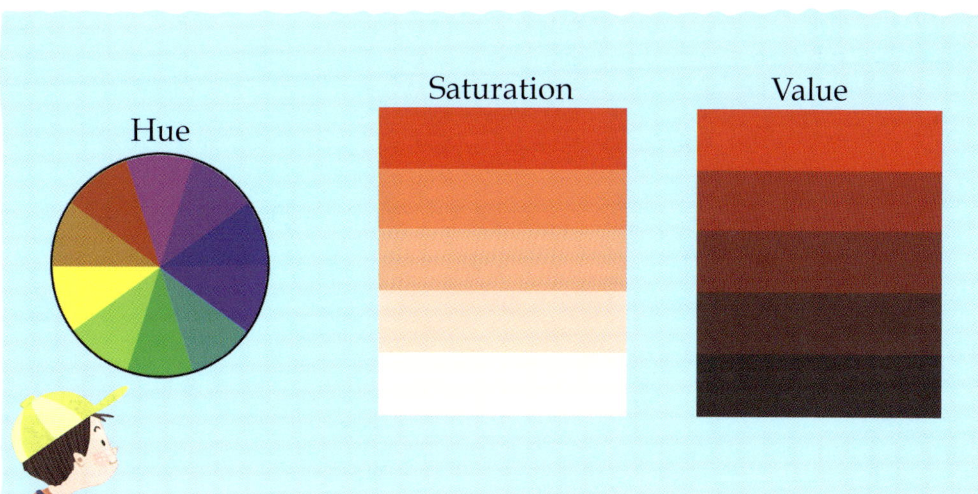

5. The Colour Wheel

The Colour Wheel was developed by Sir Isaac Newton in the form of a circular diagram in 1666. It is the basis for all colour theory and the basic tool for combining or mixing colours. It shows the relationship between colours. There are twelve basic colours that are called 'hues'. The colours can be lightened by adding white (called a 'tint') or darkened by adding black (a 'shade').

The primary, secondary and tertiary colours are all a part of the colour wheel. It has been designed in such a unique manner that any colour that you pick from it will look good.

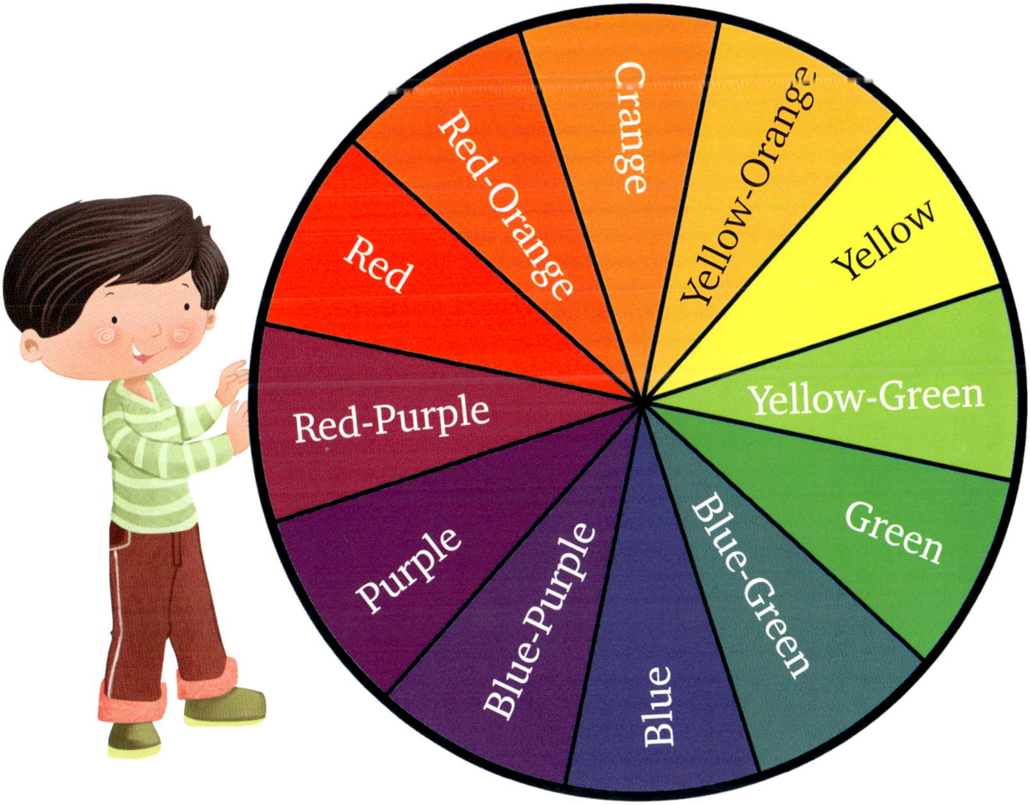

Why is the colour wheel important?

How and where you place a colour is important when you are pairing and mixing colours. Will you apply one colour or the complementary colour too? Will the surrounding hue of the colour be lighter or darker? You can take these important decisions with the help of the colour wheel as it is a powerful tool for creating eye-pleasing colour combinations for your paintings.

POCKET FACT

Black is considered as the centre of gravity in the colour wheel. It absorbs all the other colours.

A thorough knowledge of the colour wheel, and a proper understanding of the difference between primary, secondary, and tertiary colours will make your colour-mixing a lot easier. Understanding the difference between complementary, warm and cool colours is also important.

What are warm and cool colours?

The colour circle can be divided into warm and cool colours. Warm colours are energetic. Cool colours create a calm and soothing impression. White, black and grey are neutral colours, meaning they are neither warm nor cool.

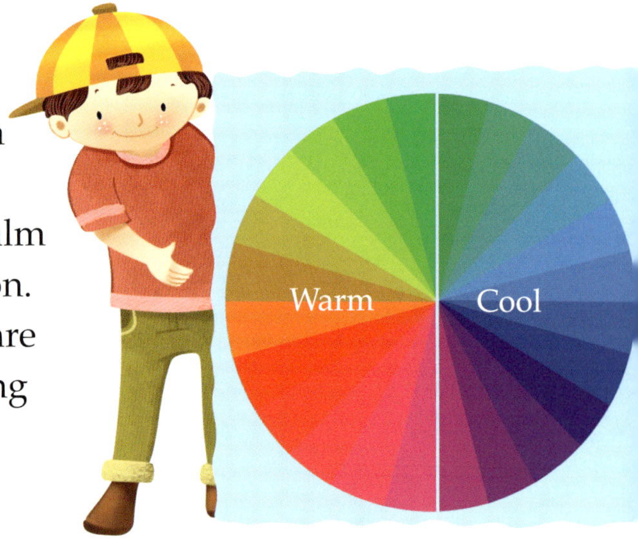

Blue and yellow, for example, both come in warm and cool hues. A cool yellow will look greenish, while a warm yellow will look orangish. Similarly, a blue that's warmer will look more purple whereas a cool blue will look more greenish.

Just like its counterparts blue and yellow, red comes in both warm and cool hues too. A warm red will look orangish, while a cool red will look purplish.

Yellow + Red = Hunger

No wonder many fast food giants as well as restaurants display this colour scheme in their advertisements. Research shows that red and yellow are the most appetising colours. Blue is the least appetising colour.

What are tints, shades and tones?

These terms sound complicated but they describe colour concepts that are simple in nature. For example, if white is used to make a colour lighter, the result is called a tint. If you add black to a colour, the darker version that is created is called a shade. The result is a different tone if you add grey to a colour.

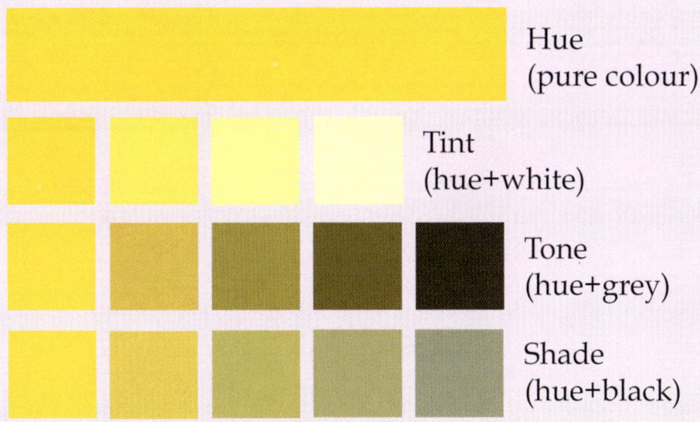

POCKET FACT

Warm colours like red, yellow, and orange display warmth because they remind us of things like the sun, heat, sunshine or fire. Cool colours like blue, green, and purple (violet) bring about a cool feeling because they remind us of things like water, sky, grass, ice and snow.

6. Mixing Primary Colours

Remember that the exact shade or tint of the secondary colour you make depends on the shade (light or dark) of your primary colour and the amount you are using. But what happens if you mix the three primary colours, that is, red, blue and yellow together?

You get black!

POCKET FACT

Three other colours can also be used to create black, although these are not primary colours. They are cyan, magenta, and yellow.

How much of each primary colour should I use?

Suppose you are creating orange, then the type of orange that you get will depend on the proportion of the red-to-yellow that you are mixing. If you use more of red than yellow in your mix, then the orange that will be created will be more of a reddish orange. But if you add more yellow than red in your final mix, then the orange created will be more of a yellowish orange.

DID YOU KNOW?

That dark grey colour that your eyes see as soon as you turn off the lights is known as 'eigengrau'.

What are pre-mixed primary colours?

Young artists have an advantage today. You can buy pre-mixed reds, blues and yellow colours and this range is wide. For example, when it comes to blue, there are colours like a stunning cobalt blue, a cool caribbean blue, a nice cerulean blue, a royal prussian blue, and a lovely sevres blue, among others. The reds include shades like cadmium red, carmine, cadmium scarlet, alizarin crimson and venetian red. Yellow is not far behind with colour ranges like naples yellow, cadmium yellow, lemon yellow and yellow ochre.

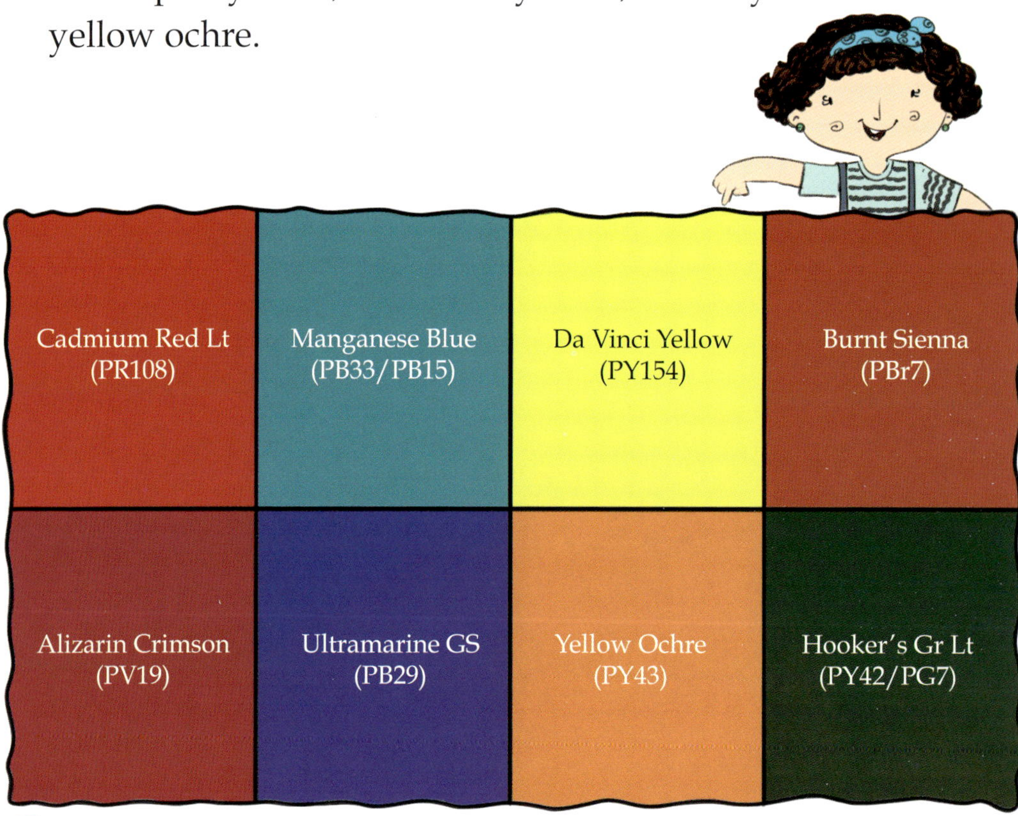

Colour Mixing Tip: Make sure that you clean your brushes with soap and water in between the mixing. This is because the paint of a previous colour might mix with the two colours you are mixing right now.

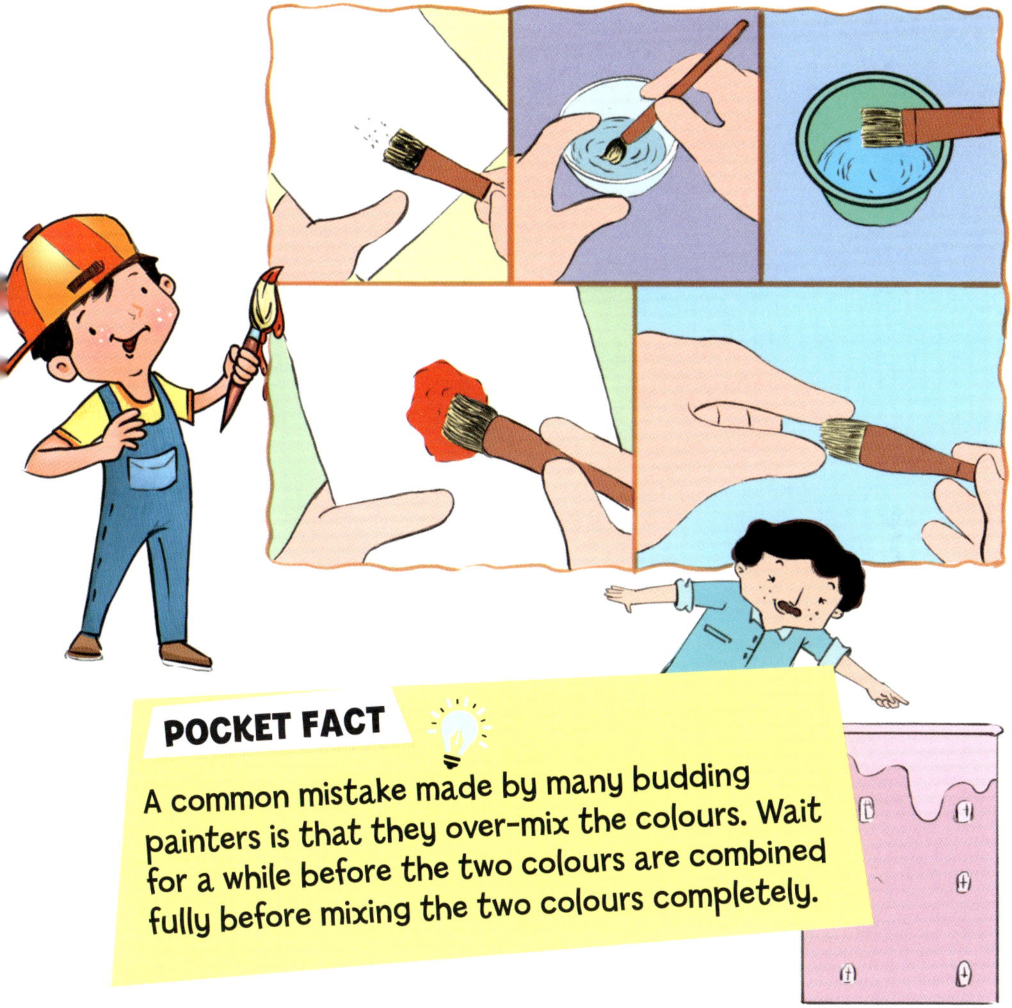

POCKET FACT

A common mistake made by many budding painters is that they over-mix the colours. Wait for a while before the two colours are combined fully before mixing the two colours completely.

7. What Are Complementary Colours

Every primary colour, that is, red, yellow, and blue has its own complementary colour that is totally exclusive. The complementary colour sits opposite its primary colour on the colour wheel. For example, the complementary colour of blue is orange, red and green are complementary colours, and so are purple and yellow. When placed side-by-side, they make the other appear brighter. This relationship of being placed opposite on the colour wheel is called '**Complementary**'.

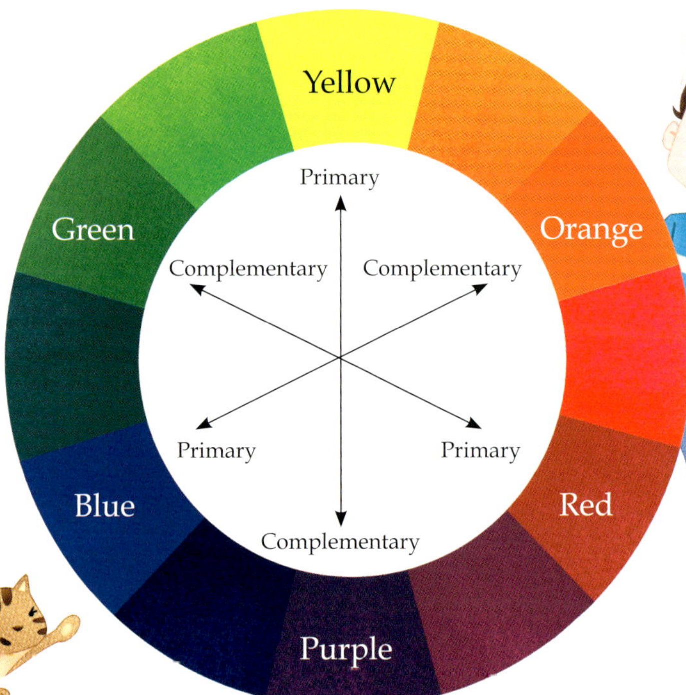

How is a complementary colour made?

The complementary colour of a primary colour is made by mixing the other two primary colours. But you need to take care when you place a primary colour next to its complementary colour. If you place red and green on a canvas, for example, this can cause a problem for someone who is seeing your painting. That is because if the complementary colours are placed next to each other, they make each other appear brighter and more intense. This creates optical distortion when viewing the painting as the wavelengths of the two colours are completely different.

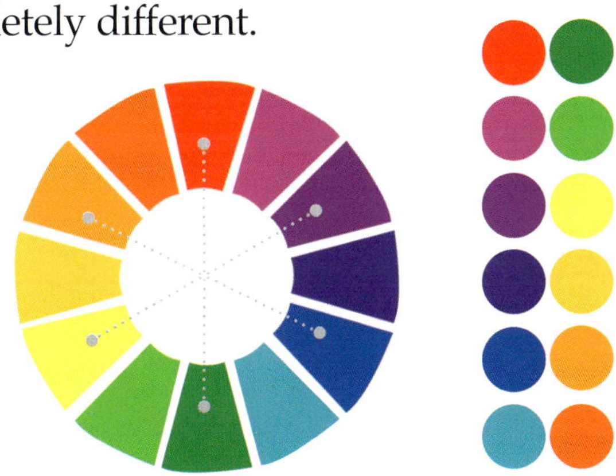

Complementary colour combinations

Colour Mixing Tip: Be patient. Practise with different amounts of paint, using different kinds of combinations. This will give you the perfect picture as to how your paints will interact with each other.

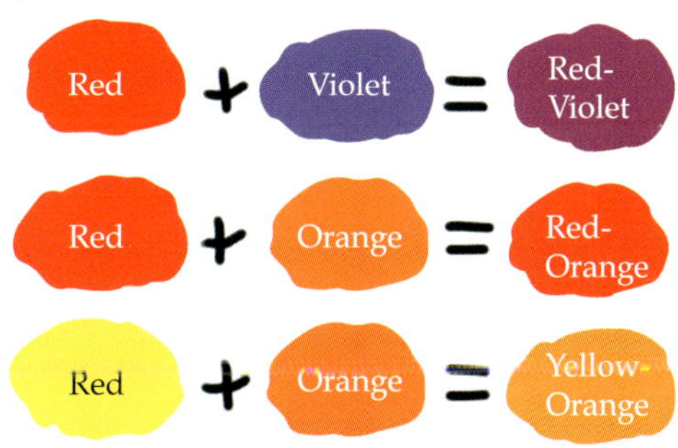

1. Identify all the three colours (the two colours that are being mixed and the third colour that is being made).

2. Write down the names of the colours of the following five objects given below.

Solve the crossword using the clues given:

Across

3 tomato

4 grapes

6 dirt

8 banana

Down

1 grass

2 pumpkin

5 street

7 sky

9 cloud

Mixing the Colours

Across

3. You get this colour by mixing red and blue

6. This is a primary colour that can be used to make orange, yellow-green, and yellow-orange

7. You get this colour by mixing red and violet

10. You get this colour by mixing yellow and orange

11. You get this colour by mixing blue and green

12. You get this colour by mixing yellow and blue

Down

1. This is a primary colour that can be used to make green, blue-violet, and blue-green

2. You get this colour by mixing yellow and green

4. You get this colour by mixing blue and violet

5. This is a primary colour that can be used to make orange, red-violet, and red-orange.

8. You get this colour by mixing red and yellow

9. You get this colour by mixing orange and red

GLOSSARY

Colour	a result of the way the object reflects or emits light
Hue	a true colour
Chroma	the Greek word for colour
Saturation	the intensity of a colour
Colour theory	the study of colour
Intensity	the brightness or degree of a colour's purity or saturation
Pure colour	not mixed with any other colour

ANSWERS

Page 28.
Red+Yellow=Orange
Red+Blue= Purple
Yellow+Blue=Green

Page 29.

Green	Pumpkin
Brown	Red
Yellow	White
Red	Yellow
Pink	

Page 30. **Across**

3. Red
4. Green
6. Brown
8. Yellow

Down

1. Green
2. Orange
5. Grey
7. Blue
9. White

Page 31. **Down**

1. Blue
2. Yellow-Green
4. Blue-Violet
5. Red
8. Orange
9. Red-Orange

Across

3. Purple
6. Yellow
7. Red-Violet
10. Yellow-Orange
11. Blue-Green
12. Green